A Thousand Tiny Awakenings

46

Library and Archives Canada Cataloguing in Publication

Title: A thousand tiny awakenings / edited by Connor Lafortune & Lindsay Mayhew.
Names: Lafortune, Connor, editor. | Mayhew, Lindsay, editor.
Identifiers: Canadiana (print) 20250112043 | Canadiana (ebook) 20250112051 | ISBN 9781988989884
(softcover) | ISBN 9781988989891 (EPUB)
Subjects: LCSH: Oppression (Psychology)—Poetry. | CSH: Canadian poetry (English)—21st century. |
LCGFT: Poetry.
Classification: LCC PS8287.O67 T56 2025 | DDC C811/.6080353—dc23

Printed and bound in Canada on 100% recycled paper.
Cover Artwork: Grant Neegan
Cover Design: Heather Campbell

Published by:
Latitude 46 Publishing
info@latitude46publishing.com
Latitude46publishing.com

We acknowledge the support of the Ontario Arts Council and the Canada Book Fund for their generous financial support.

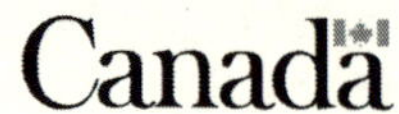

A Thousand Tiny Awakenings

Edited by Connor Lafortune & Lindsay Mayhew

"We have to create. It is the only thing louder than destruction."
— Andrea Gibson, *Take Me With You*

"What if I wrote something that sounded like dozens of people in protest?"
— Billy-Ray Belcourt, *A Minor Chorus*

Table of Contents

A Note from the Editors 1

Whispers of Threads 3
Waed Hasan

Pain in Purpose - A Journey of Rediscovery 6
Chimdi Kingsley-Emereuwa

Indians In The Making 8
Connor Lafortune

Happiness is a Warm Dog 11
Nicole Robitaille

28 Days of Compassion 13
Ra'anaa Yaminah Ekundayo

Wovenness 15
Sydney Read

Feeling is an Organ is a Symphony 17
Lindsay Mayhew

Heterodoxy 19
Sydney Read

Schrödinger's Casket 22
Kay Kassirer

Twenty Eight Days. 24
Carson Bohdi

Cruci(pre)fix 25
Lindsay Mayhew

The Sharpest Tongue 29
Connor Lafortune

i am living by the minute 34
Lisa Shen

Wanderers 35
Tyler Hein

Tacklebox Daydream. 39
Michelle Delorme

to be a Tree 41
Blaine Thornton

Meteor Fragmenting 45
Lindsay Mayhew

The Dimensions of Bodies Kept Afloat 48
Jesse June-Jack

Home 51
Brennan Gregoire

Rabbits Chasing Tail 58
Connor Lafortune

The Dragon 62
Ra'anaa Yaminah Ekundayo

Firestorm 64
Michelle Delorme

In The Aftermath of Apocalypse 65
Connor Lafortune and Lindsay Mayhew

Acknowledgments 69

Author Bios 71

A Note from the Editors

Oppression takes many forms. It manifests in ways that are violent, pervasive, and haunting. *A Thousand Tiny Awakenings* unites young and marginalized voices to subvert the structures of oppression that continue to pervade our lives. Although the authors reside all over Turtle Island, this collection is curated and published on the traditional lands of the Atikameksheng Anishnawbek and the traditional lands of the Wahnapitae First Nation on the Robinson Huron Treaty Territory of 1850.

This project, at its core, seeks to uplift the voices of the upcoming generation in their journey to dismantle and break boundaries that track lines across their bodies, lives, relationships, and futures.

Our art is resistance.

Our poetry is resurgence.

Our stories are a call to action and a testimony to our collective, breathtaking resiliency.

Our words are revolution.

Connor Lafortune & Lindsay Mayhew

Whispers of Threads

Waed Hasan

I

t-o   r - u - n //
                From   &   Towards//
once to the w a t e r   now within the silhouettes of this house //
it // follows // us //
                Not how a heart goes to a wandering child //
                 nor how the birds know their way home //

// We are the pause   between b r e a t h s
Invisible threads t-e-t-h-e-r-i-n-g us to uncertainty //
    A mirror held to a fragmented world // Each line a boundary, yet a bridge

// Time, a labyrinth
                                we
                    navigate
                                                        blindly
               Walls of solitude, windows to introspection //
               In the cadence of empty streets, hope resides //

// So we move //
                From   &   Towards//
T-o-r-u-n's voice echoes, faint but clear //
From isolation's cocoon, transformation emerges //

In frag   Mente
                d line s, t
                      he hu   man   spirit   pe   rseveres //

II

And then,

Smoke

Rubble

Bodies.

Beirut is weeping. A city laid bare.

The sky here is fractured Breathe in . hold .
Breathe out .

Hold .

• •

• •

Breathe in . hold . Breathe out . Hold .

The explosion's touch a brutal art Behind the eyes
a canvas of anguish

unfurls

What once was now torn apart Here, the tether
pulls from within,

yearning

In the ashes we wait Remember the streets,
Remember the

buildings

For the city to rise Two worlds apart

A phoenix of hope. **

III

Re.verse

/rə'vərs,'rēvərs/

To move backwards.

1. Before the heat came
   They'd carve their names into trees
   Lovers, waiting for the birds to come home.

2. When the pebbles don't skip – just fall
   The children do not know how to swim
   Remember, how the rivers yearned?

3. Time does not move backwards
   We cannot drive forward in reverse
   Imagine, if we knew this before we got here.

4. Nothing left to burn.

O.ver

/'ōvər/

Beyond and falling.

Pain in Purpose - A Journey of Rediscovery

Chimdi Kingsley-Emereuwa

The vain reality of survival in a post radical
world is the genesis of the monsters hiding
underneath societal norms and power

Make a man out of a scarred
boy you get yourself a broken society

Well, Papa ain't raise no
fool he said, to take no
prisoners so I am ready to throw a fist

But Mama taught me to say
prayer when I hit rock bottom

My knees hit the floor in humility
palms clapped together, eyes closed and
I call on the Lord's name with my burning lips

I smoke my words out down to a mere
vapor turn my prayers into poem shredding its vulnerability

Confessing how my faith runs like
water and oil refusing to mix
I cry to the Lord

Even though my song
is fading, I am still worthy of a dance

And just like that I count myself
blessed among men, giving these poems
a part of me that are only discovered

Through meticulous soul-searching, I am no longer
    afraid of the destruction that comes with becoming

There comes a momentary
    lapse of fulfillment; saying good
    riddance to bad rubbish

Afterall, I have mastered how to wear my
    pain, like a crown of royalty, so people desire it

Maybe just this once we won't ask to be more but
    celebrate everything we were before acceptance
    becomes a placebo for our pain

Every pill swallowed an
    ode to broken trust and renewed hopes

A catharsis for rediscovery we
    shall then dare to celebrate the
    salvation of what could have been
Rising above the powers that be.

Indians In The Making

Connor Lafortune

In Thomas King's 2012 novel "The Inconvenient Indian: A Curious Account of Native People in North America" he describes Indigenous people according to the categories of the Dead, Live, and Legal Indian. Here is how I understand those Indians, and their Palatable cousin today.

The Dead Indian wears a golden moose-hide leather vest, copper-coloured war paint over his eyes, and two braids flowing down to his chest, an eagle feather resting between their intersection. His bone bead breast plate rests all the way to his hips, hiding his bare chest and healed-over scars. He walks around town with a loin cloth and moccasins; forgets he lives in Northeastern Ontario now and ignores the breeze. He approaches the crowd waiting for coffee at Timmies and says "Today is a good day to die." And he does, he did; *die* I mean. A long time ago, before his story even began. He lives within the walls of museums, in Western films repeated in old-folks' homes, within stories told only of the past. His life, beside other Warriors whose names we can only recall the shape of. He lives inside of us too; buried beneath our t-shirts and jeans, behind the snapback hats and glasses, just beyond the highway. He doesn't come close to us anymore. Says it's too dangerous to die a second time.

The Living Indian shows up early to the zoom call. Wears his hair in a long braid you can barely see on screen. He sits before a wall of medicine. Mashkiki he uses to clean out what his Western world puts in him. You see him with a tree and think he's one with the earth. He is; *but not because you think it.* His water bottle is covered with stickers that let you know he is not fucking around. To you, he's just an activist; to him, it's simply living. He brews your discomfort and lets you seep in it. Sips on it when he sits in class. Disrupts every lecture on capitalism to scream about the crisis still going on in Oka, and Thunder Bay, and Kenora, and on and on and on. When he looks in the mirror, his hair unbraids. His hands soften as he undoes the bolo from his neck. *He cannot be seen like this.* He tucks his hair under a ball cap, throws on a t-shirt with old jogging pants from the laundry pile. He breaks the mirror. *He can't see himself like this.* He removes the Keith Secola CD from his car, connects his bluetooth instead. Takes the sweetgrass braid from the dash and throws it in the backseat. A group of men walk out of the arena in headdresses; the white of their skin painted to match their favorite teams' jerseys. Their war cries echo in the distance. He thinks, "real Indians are dead, living ones can't be Indian" as he drives off into the sunset.

The Legal Indian steps up to the office dressed in a suit and tie. His hair braided and slicked back with bear grease, it whips as he struts to the desk. He wears black dress shoes, beaded with the finest of hands, presses his status card to the desk and says "I am here to collect my treaty pay." The desk clerk still says no.

The Palatable Indian walks into the classroom with short spiked hair done up with gel instead of bear grease. He leaves his moccasins at home by the door and wears Nikes instead. He has a medicine wheel pin on his jacket; small enough to ignore. He is quiet; funny; friendly. Never yells unless it is by a rink. He smells of ax body spray with a hint of burnt sage; most people assume he smokes. He doesn't correct them. He lives in the city. He has only ever driven past a moose. He mumbles to himself when he's nervous. His friends assume he is speaking the language; they listen more intently. He finishes with "ahô" so they stop listening. They write fiction around him as he does nothing but smile:

"He does sweats all the time; real sacred!"

"His grandmother married the chief!"

"His Indian name means eagle!"

"Why can't they all be like him!"

All the while he chuckles; thinking to himself, "If only they knew." Becomes embodied practice instead.

I've come to realize that every horror movie is a Black and Indigenous reality. We have lived through genocide, ongoing apocalypse, and famine. We have been the vampires with our heads cut off and burned at the stake, the zombies walking around with diseases left without a cure, the misunderstood shapeshifter seeking shelter. We have been the invisible man trying to get someone to hear him, the quiet village trying not to make a sound, the screaming body in asylum. We have seen the ending of them all. The colonial agenda seeks to keep us all in a perpetual state of fear and confrontation. While they occupy us with preventing our destruction, we cannot overcome our place in society. We are left to fight each other instead.

The **Dead Indian** confines us to the past;

The **Live Indian** is removed from Indigeneity;

The **Legal Indian** is given a name from faceless dolls.

love is not always political

Indigenous love is, though

the way it bends into something **Palatable**

just to poison the meal

Happiness is a Warm Dog

Nicole Robitaille

Cookie, the young bloodhound,
    gets his teeth brushed this Monday morning
    by his loving owner, who must pass
    the time before removing her roller set
    (resting safely under her hair cap)
    to see if the overnight magic
    transformed afro curls into fine ringlets.

Cookie's canines
    glisten after
    rinsing, a reminder of his breeding,
    those years of careful mating to have
    a bite strong enough to break bone
    and flesh.
    Grooming him, carefully
    like polishing
    a pearl.

    His ancestor
Persephone, a plantation dog from a
history-chained country, tracked muddy footprints
through her master's manor and barked at every
Black who crossed the boundary
from the field to the yard.

    Before she was free to roam the property,
Persephone was trained to stay in the field, bound and whipped.
Day by day, a seed of anger
germinated within her, left to gnash
her teeth, growl,
flying spit at her tormentor
greedy for his blood.

His dark skin was marked with her bites
as he lifted his whipping hand, raised
by an invisible rein held by his master,
the threat of death tightening his chest.

In the moment he hesitates
then strikes the whip against the bloodhound,
binding their submission,
her bark echoing generations after.

Far from the sound of whip and bark –

Cookie is
pampered with a pedicure
(toes cleaned, nails trimmed, head kissed)
his hair, healthy and shining
after conditioning with $20 soap.

He returns his owner's love
with a lick. She brushes his hooded cape
of black fur, speaks as tenderly
as a mother in her baby-voice affections
complimenting his
glossy coat of bloodhound fur

once
combed by the master
who would beckon Persephone to rest in his lap,
grooming her as carefully as one would polish a gun.

28 Days of Compassion

Ra'anaa Yaminah Ekundayo

February is Black History Month

And while I exist year round, for these next four weeks they tell me I truly matter

I am tired.
I am spread thin.
I am exploited for labour
and knowledge that they then
refuse to acknowledge.

Some days I can't respond to an email.
Some days I can't respond to a text.
Some days I can't hold a conversation because all my strength
is spent holding my head high.

I see how they look through me;
classmates, and colleagues, and strangers on the street.
Before their eyes, a commodification,
a hypersexualized being, nameless in the face of *his* story

Stolen by "saviours"
Pushed to the peripheries

Beaten and broken, bound and shackled
Beaten and broken, bound and shackled

The burden of my existence plagues me
If I join the race, they move the finish line
And if I stand still, they build boundaries upon my bare Black back

How can you pick yourself up from your bootstraps when
you have no shoes?
How can you turn the other cheek when your face is swollen

beyond recognition?
How can you fear us when our hands are trembling in the air?

Time and time again...

Feel me pull away at the sound pleasantries
Flinch at the stench of performance
And falter in the face of an ugly power

Oh, we *see* you
Oh, we *hear* you
Oh, we *feel* you

I exist year round

February is Black History Month
Save your 28 days of compassion

Me nah work for free, massa

Wovenness

Sydney Read

two snakes
in breaths of each other
passed over the asphalt
before me

the first, long and lean and little lifted her
head looking
ahead of herself, ignoring me who

was but passing before her
passing near her
she was feeding warm earth to her
water-belly

loving how it
melded with her water motions
and i
marveled
at her

mind
i wished she wasn't
leaving me
behind

though i
moved on i began to crave
the sun-soaked dirt
in the earth in

my belly, wide and water-full from
the earth

and then
he
slid onto the asphalt stopping to
turn his eyes his tongue toward
me, i wonder if i smelled like
sun or silicon if i was
water-wrong but
i walked beside him anyway
remembering what it means to be
a woman and a snake
i wonder if he
remembers me in his water-belly in his
yellow-striped sides that slink along the ground remembering what
he

is to the earth if
he
knows that he and i and she
must stop and see each other
seeing each other

we know

we are water-bellied
Otherworlds
and one day we will meet
to give thanks
and eat our tails (together)
in gratitude
for the knowledge
of abyss.

Feeling is an Organ is a Symphony

Lindsay Mayhew

i wonder why Anger is self-destructive
/ ex(in)terior / i chart Anger's dimensions and find them to be multiple
/ mutations /
spiteful verses and voices spark fires in my Ears /
my Face burns / Eyes twitch /
scraps of my Hair slither on the bathroom tiles / i break /
my Knuckles on the dash of my car / i snap / pencils over my Kneecaps /
i eat / away at the only thing i have control over /
i am acid and liberation / and some nights it
feels like my Skin is the only thing stopping me from being free /
disillusioned / if only i
could / scoop out my Organs / hang them on the clothesline / sapped
and sundried /

i daydream Anger / to be a calculated strike / a jailbreak / a forest fire
that fosters
new growth
or something neat and dazzling like that
these fantasies rescue Anger from avenues of smallness / zones of irrelevance /
but i am conditioned to be reason / able / solid / pacified

i have so much Anger and no where to put it except
this /object\ of a Body
a lot of nights i am defined: pathetic
i just cry
and cry
cry because Anger has nowhere else to go but skyward / bursting
that's why i re / define Anger as righteous / shooting out towards the
heavens / breaking its gravitational pull / parting the curtains of the galaxy
you forget that biblical angels aren't made of silk and honey / they are
terrifying /
that's what this Anger ought to be /
a brutal winged thing / Mouthless, feathered, petrifying / a thousand
Eyes / blinking /

appearing in dreams / streets / drains / following, taunting, waiting / that's what this Anger is /
a feral rage / an ancient combustion / because / become / because
isn't madness historically woman ? / isn't hysteria in my Blood ? / don't we haunt
    haunt
    haunt
the world / still ?
                                        / when i write it out / there is something so sublime / beautiful / about the way we bend / break / i think because it feels like a whale song / a call reverberating in a sea of temporal / pulling lineage up from the cacophony of the earth's core / feeling / is an Organ / is a symphony
                our disconnection, a web
finding our vibrational bearings in each other's agony
                                                    / after all / isn't Anger just Desire
denied?   isn't shame just / another name for possibility ?
/ this current within me rushes at the touch of Skin /
i am not afraid to beg for love / potential liberty

so i brush Fingertips and rupture all at once / press Chests and perforate
                                    / clasp Palms and
                            break shards of myself into the sea
                        come back on shore with smoother edges
/ collected / and rendered
into stain glass tombstone with inscriptions of vengeance / and Healing

Heterodoxy

Sydney Read

take this and eat of it   this is My Body
this is My Blood
it was given up   (*because of*) for you

take My Body for your body

as wine-blood as body-bread and remember **I** made
you
have
never
been in my image what is
your image?
i take my
body
of
bodyblood, breadwine

take this and eat of ***me***   **I** AM

picking the scabs off my chest to check
my flesh and see what
folds of bread, what flowing wine i ate on
(fed on)
so i might Become You
Become...

at night i stood/   stand in front of the mirror and the shower steams
i peel my banana-self i drop my clothes on the floor and watch misty folds
of flesh bleed like wine
i used to do this/   i do this i do this *i do this*
i used to look
(i am looking)
in my flesh

for Your Flesh
In my breadwine bloodybody
what i mean is
i wish i was better
i wish/ed You made me better
so
i made me better
i put my body/my toes into soil
to feel within to feel a part of
something greater than You, a Body that necessitated (birthed) You

i should sway as a willow
melt into moss and Sky and drink on sip on
Her Blood
but
i am not whimsical
i don't stand in sinful sunflowers or stand still
in cold altar-lines (hands folded)
nor do i
trip in tents to praise the Sky
(Her Blood!)
i do. i do hope. i do pour myself out when i
see stars.
but i see window-sun shadows on the kitchen floor. i pray for my eyes (i am)
On the kitchen floor i
turn (sunflower!) outward i try
to spill
myself like a chalice
Out (of You)
Into place
Within place

i try to **Be** (Become! Become! Become!)
In Place.

to be water over the blood in my body and its wrong wrong wrongness
now i don't pray, only try

i want to be the Space
Between
the stain glass window and the
                                        wafer grasped by my five-year old grimy-grim fingers
the light that basks within, that knows, that tells:

"Digest.
Pass on."

Schrödinger's Casket

Kay Kassirer

in judaism it is a sin to kill myself
my body belongs
to god
so suicide is seen as stealing something
that is not mine
as if the sun could steal moonlight

this isn't the first time
I have been told that a man
has more authority over my body
than I do

I'm not saying that god is a man
just that I had to call them one
in synagogue when I prayed

hebrew, a gendered language
god,
recipient of masculine conjugations
and gendered congregations

the talmud acknowledges the existence of more than two sexes
but when I visit my friend's orthodox synagogue
before we enter
we both pause
unsure of which section to sit in
then find our
selves separated by the mechitza
divided
into binary genders we don't fit in

a few hours away from where that friend lives
a shooter opens fire at a synagogue in pennsylvania
named L'Simcha

                    Tree of Life
                            becomes burial ground for bullet

not even synagogue is safe
        isolating women to the back of the shul
                    ignoring nonbinary existence in our scripture

rebbetzin is the hebrew word for female rabbi
but a dictionary will tell you it means rabbi's *wife*

my mother took me to a reconstructionist chavurah
        taught me that rules are made to be played with
                    that women are allowed to be rabbis
                    that my body belongs to myself and *no one else*

my mother's medically assisted death
is a jewish schrodinger's casket
except there is no need to take the lid off the box
        my mother both *did* and *did not* kill herself

        she always was one to fuck around with god

Twenty Eight Days

Carson Bohdi

It was a Sunday, at twilight,
my eyes locked on the ceiling lit in *crimson,*
as pain implodes my abdomen.
I fight, *denial, anger, shame…*
until the dawn breaks, I break,
and I surrender to **my body, a cage…**
one I wish I could escape.
As the sun breaks through the skyline
I ache, *in twenty eight ways.*

Picture this; feeling a dagger twisting and turning no matter the medicine you take as

your mind begins to race, and your skin begins to **rage;**

And yet, here I lay, on Sunday, at twilight,
every twenty eight days…

Cruci(pre)fix

Lindsay Mayhew

poems are the only place i still commune with god.

i was the plant that grew
skewed
onlookers wonder what went wrong
with the girl grown up *godly*

i am shedding leaves
ridding myself of rot
becoming a rhizome of roots

when the sun is high &
the time is right
i will come alive
i don't really exist yet
but i am longing to

even now
every prayer reads
like barbwire braille
fingers spilling carnage
bloody
trailing mahogany
across the phantom of my body
whore is a legacy
leaving acid on my lips
pesticide
churning shame & bile in my gut
every word stumbling
out of my mouth
reeks of it

How to think of Body when Language is rooting against you

in
the blinding
white glow of the cross
i slip
backwards
tumbling down black rabbit holes
grabbing onto loose soil
coming up empty handed
soiled
(soiled soiled soiled soiled soiled soiled soiled soiled)

i ask not to be thrown among the waste.

(I HAVE SAID THE WORD BODY IN ALL 7139 LANGUAGES
THEY ALL FELT UNFAMILIAR ON MY TONGUE
BUT ONLY ENGLISH FELT LIKE
A STRANGER)
poems are second comings multiple
worlds 0 bound
1 less
(re) // (in) 0 coded capacities
surrections 0 dialects indistinct
1
0
that's all it takes t0 make a language
1
with crooked fingers
i will
shoot out through miles of earth
webbing & tangling & flowing & fragmenting
seeking a time where i am loved,
always
searching
slip
ping
backwards forwards

the world tells me to stop playing god.
so now i only play Poet.

i will not
entomb this body
for the world
i become poem
&
(re) // (de)
construct the page

i am
writing a body
that looks like connections
not leftovers
stitching these wounds to feel
utopian
ineverconclude

blood letting ink onto paper
bending bones into line
breaks
skin s t r e t c h i n g
bleeding
extending into syntax

i infect the meaning
of (bound)aries // viral
save the sentiments i want to keep
& fuck the rest
re // collect

(un)write

I WRITE A BODY FULL OF OPENINGS /
NOT EXITS
A BODY NAMED MIDDLE
WHERE DISTINCTION COMES TO DIE /
DIE /
DIE

A BODY THAT GIVES
ALL
(AND LOSES NOTHING)
DISPERSING INTO EVERYTHING
REMADE FROM ROOTS & L1NKS
1 (re)MEMBER THIS BODY AS
WOR1D-MAKER

0   1 00
0 0 re / write
dis / write   0   1
0   1   0   / disa / vow(e)l 0
1 1 cons / onant // tent
dis / embowel 0 1

dis / re / un / in / non
tangle together in liminal spaces
disi**re****am**un**somewhere**in**between**non

my beating heart, waiting
beneath a foxglove
)*blooming blooming blooming blooming blooming blooming blooming*(
for a future
i can one day
become

The Sharpest Tongue

Connor Lafortune

it didn't always hurt like this
        to speak
                      I mean
or maybe I was just better at hiding the pain

                                        n   a   i   v   e

I suppose

I don't remember the blood
                      just the taste of it
I used to wake up with bruises
the
        size
                      of
                                    Worlds
on my palms

I never thought I would let   go

at night, it spilt onto my sheets
I   spoke   sentences   into   existence
let the excess flow passed my teeth

        my teeth
were still so white when I looked in the mirror

                          what does that tell you about my body?

I got so used to that taste of cotton on my tongue
that I began to eat them like marshmallows

their sweetness
                          p   e   r   m   e   a   t   e   d

the pennies tucked between each tooth

now
I can't look at medicine cabinets
without thinking of maps
leading anywhere but home

...

I have always spoken my mother's tongue
my fathers too I suppose
never my grandmothers
she was never given one to speak from

always mute
always left with so much
she
could
not
say

always left on days I felt our heart beat as one
one day she will remember
I hoped
I hope she remembers

those days when language was the only
d i s t a n c e
between us

I would ask for du lait
she would hand me milk
just the same

I spoke just the same
way her husbands did
her children too

she believed my tongue would soften like theirs had

it never did

it gets caught on every tooth now

they have sharpened themselves with every word
I never learnt as a child

nimaamaa
indede
daga
gaawin onjidaa

gaawin onjidaa I am sorry

I would have apologized sooner

if only I knew how

...

la francophonie
une langues p ointu
a iguille
c oupante
mais seulement parfois
seul ce contexte peut être

des mot donné en cadeau
maman
papa
frère
chien
cadeaux

ces moins qui sembles être adoucie au point
mais seulement parfois
seul ce contexte peut être

ma langue, attacher
en
noeud
maintenant
impossible de les d é f a i r e s

...

french is the first language I spoke
then english
then something resembling the past
something resembling home perhaps
mais seulement parfois
seul ce contexte peut être

...

I speak in tongues now
I am a traveler seeking to learn the language of
my
blood
my blood
the only thing reminding me of home

the only taste that reminds me of my grandmother
walking with me along the shore

animose noongom
she walks away now
never learnt to follow language

this one at least

she doesn't hear my calls
indaashaan
gego maajaa
gego ninaganaa

my tongue has softened grandmother
just not the way you intended
I am learning the words you were never given
as a child

I am giving them to you as a gift

nokomis

gizaagi'

miinigoowizi

nigiiwe

I go home when I think of you
I think of home when I look into my blue eyes

b l u ee y e s

the shores you have gifted me
I walk along them every day

there are no more pennies
no more cotton caught between my teeth

my palms are empty now

I will be here when you are ready
to let go of your mother's words
the world you have in your hands

when you are ready

I will be here

I will answer
your calls

i am living by the minute

Lisa Shen

when the days are too much to carry,
i carve time into sand grains.

in one, i am sitting on the porch,
watching starlings scatter the dawn.

in another, i am spooning honey into tea,
sucking on a slice of lemon.

and yes, there are the moments that stretch long as the night, when all the skeletons rise to knock on my closet door, and i find myself kneeling over my grave plot, begging the soil to turn over —

but in this one,
i am gathering wildflowers from the meadow,

lying on a sea of grass,
watching airplanes wink into stars.

i move through time as steady as my heart beats,
as sure as breath and tide —

once .

then again .

and

again

.

Wanderers

Tyler Hein

Tell me why my thoughts always jump to the end. You sprint into the Fred Starr Legion stinking of peat and drugstore perfume, unable to even fool yourself with your announcement that this stay is a permanent one. You've been on edge since returning from an autumn spent harvesting cranberries, in Quebec - *Saint-Louis-de-Blandford* - you clarify. The language tumbles clumsily from your mouth, half-learned and unearned. It sounds so strange to hear your voice lacking certainty, like a flame without heat.

The tender plops a pitcher between us. You thank him in French, and he responds in the only language he knows. I pour the pilsner into pint glasses still dewy from the wash. We watch the generous head froth and settle in a silence you puncture within a minute with greedy reminiscing about the cranberry bogs. Workers flooding whole fields for the cranberries to float upon, how the sun could never warm the blood-thick water, so you'd shiver when plodding through the mire, pushing berries into a bucket, how the wolf spiders who resided in the vines escaped drowning by scampering up your body, hundreds at a time. Your hands add fitful herky-jerky flourishes to the stories, spilling more than you drink. Your foot jitters against the floorboards, sticky with soapy beer.

"That sounds horrifying."

No, you declare. *They keep the berries clean. We treat them as coworkers... I lied earlier. I think. I didn't mean to lie, but I lied. I think. Why wouldn't I go back? It's my dream job. What's your dream job?*

"I don't dream of labour."

You roll your eyes and chuckle through a few exaggerated nods. *Well, I've found my calling.* I mimic your nod. The same as a thief believing everyone steals, I'm confident you're lying.

You said the same the March you spent posting updates from all the name-brand cities in Europe. Always out of frame was your accompaniment.

Or rather, you were his. The older man, the so-called nice, lonely man, who paid the bill in Paris, in Amsterdam, in Prague in exchange for a young and lively companion. We all knew better than to dig further when you returned without the same opinion of the man and only wore sweaters during the muggy summer. The latter trait—a concealment of skin—was absorbed into your identity. You're wearing a moss-green beanie, a thin black-and-white striped long sleeve below paint-stained denim overalls, vaguely reminiscent of the rubber suits you must have worn while wading through the quagmire you call a dream. The past sticks to you. I guess that's how it is for everyone. We're all incomplete people with complex personalities built from whichever spare parts and loose sentiment that collects on our soles during a lifetime of wandering to arrive where we'll one day die.

There's an unexplainable nature of a world in your stories I can't put a frame around in my mind that, coupled with seeing you, makes me think of infinity, which then has me feeling miniscule and unnecessary. A single grain of sand on an empty stretch of beach or a puddle slowly evaporating from the hole it fills in the cracked concrete of a service station.

Having never once encountered a quiet you weren't desperate to fill, you fidget uncomfortably across the table. Years ago, I realized that, when left to linger, silence breeds sadness in you, bleeds secrets.

I think we're made to expand, you half-shout. *To fill ourselves so large with life and stories that we must tell them again and again to stop from bursting.*

"How can you do it?"

Do what? What do you mean? How can I do what?

"How can you not know what you're coming home to? When will you know you've found what you're chasing?"

A wayward strand of anger hitches along your words. *Who says I'm chasing anything?*

"I just thought..."

We can't all be you.

I sip defensively on my beer, my shoulders bowed inward. As with seemingly every moment in my life, I have a strong impetus to apologize.

Were there only two directions in life people our age could choose? Regular people, normal people, with parents who have easily described professions, fathers who shower after work rather than before. If so, did I miss the switching track? I have the safety of a partner and an apartment with clutter and a calendar on my fridge that tracks the slow end of a year that felt quicker than the last. You have the glamor and mystique of strangers and a passport covered in stamps.

Tell me how you're able to live like an echo. To be here now and then, a while afterwards, briefly return, only fainter, each time a little less full. The only certainty is that you'll invite me out each time you return from your latest sally into another life. I'm your release valve to keep all the life you've captured from growing too large and splitting you open.

I didn't mean that, you say. *Well, I did. It's true. But I didn't mean it...*
I think you know.
I'm not brave enough to live like you.

My laugh is awkward, humourless. "Excuse me? Can you repeat that?"

It's true.

I speak through pursed lips, "I spend one half of each day talking about the other half of the day, and you have the nerve to call me brave?"

It's true.

"That's enough." I throw back the remaining beer in my glass and drop a twenty for the tender. You stand from your seat and do the same with your glass. This is your least favourite part. You've never wanted even the worst nights to end.

Outside the Starr the streets are silent with an eerie suburban calm. I scuff my shoe against the asphalt while we pretend to analyze a mural celebrating air force veterans painted on the Legion wall. Two beers were enough for me to think poetic so their faces can't help but make me wonder if all we have in common now is our past.

Though I want to ask you to stay, I can't. The word bounces around in my head in a painful spiral and brings tears to the corners of my eyes. *Stay.* It is the loneliest sound in the world when asked of someone who won't.

We hug for so long it stops hurting.

Then you say something that makes me question whether I even know you at all.

Tell me... tell me that one day I'll find some sliver in the world to call my own.

Tacklebox Daydream

Michelle Delorme

Sunlight bounces off snow and sturdy ice
to caress wind-bitten cheeks and chapped lips.
Creaking beneath our feet,
ice has been speaking to the land since the beginning of time
chatter, engraved in memory.

Mittens carve into snowcrust
the perfect shape of the moon.
An ice auger creates a looking glass into the dark world below,
fishhooks glittering on their way down.
Gripped tight against the gravitational pull, a rusty red ladle reveals frigid waters.

Tethered between worlds by a single fishing line
I am hooked on walleye, yellow perch, and Northern pike
and this wide open, snow covered ice.

Does this winter feel warmer than the last?

Dreams of thick ice and fish scales
melt away into a ribbon of grief.
Ice sheets break and thin,
fading out of existence.
Boats float on the horizon instead of ice huts, well into the winter.

I think I understand what melting feels like.
The blinding heat of the sun behind closed eyes
the drip...
drip...
                drip... of time,
counting down the days I have left.

Shrunk down, bonds broken
as my entire molecular structure is rearranged.

Separated from parts of myself.
Holding onto ice until I am cracked in half

and submerged,

eroded into warm waves of meltwater
and deep currents of temperature memory.

to be a Tree

Blaine Thornton

If I concentrate hard enough, I can make the trees breathe. I sit still and stare at a half-dead pine across the river. The branches follow my breath, expanding on the inhale and shrinking on the exhale. At this moment, I know that we are both alive. Even though the pine's bark is turning grey, a few green needles cling for life. I have been staring for so long, I am not sure if the pine is moving or if I just want it to bend so badly.

If I was a tree, I could watch the years pass through my permanent plot. I would become a fixture amongst the moving. I wish to be a bush tree with branches that hold robin nests and spiderwebs. In my grouping of life, we would dance in the wind:

bending birch trees gymnasts,
pine needles fall while shimmying,
birds would sing our praises.

A tree is exempt from human worry:
no feet to move,
no rent to pay,
no warmth to find.

Still, all tree lives come to an end. I wonder, what would be my tree tragedy? Cut with an axe for being in the wrong place? Struck by lightning for growing too tall?

I think of Hometown's trees, they are still young; the old ones were burnt in roast yards to smelt ore. Before moving, I had only known trees I could wrap my arms around. In City, trees are sparse, but I admire the width of trunks – oak trees twist sidewalks or threaten to collapse on buildings. Amongst the shouts and sirens, the lucky few have seen evolution. I suppose it would be interesting to be a City tree, to watch a City be built around me. What a heartbreaking movie that must be.

No one dares to eat the fruit from the apple tree on City street corner, the poisoned apples fall to the sidewalk and rot.

I stand by a mural titled, *Remember Honest Ed's.* The Pokémon Go app is the only reason I notice it. The paint on the mounted wooden board is chipping. I spin the PokéStop in an attempt to commemorate the loss of affordable housing. I wonder how the trees feel about Honest Ed's disappearing.

Maybe the oak watched it be birthed
and bulldozed.

City trees must fear death; their own shortcoming but also the falling of friends. Did the old oaks sing a poignant song as condos were born on deathbeds of siblings?

I have decided I hate City. Well, that is not totally true – I just long for swimmable lakes and a kind smile holding the door for you. I watch the sheltered ignore the unhoused without thinking twice ; I watch the houseless become ghosts ; I watch people losing their dignity.

Where do people go if we keep building unaffordable boxes in the sky?
Or fences?

If I am choosing a tree that is most like me, it would be a stressed birch: tall, fragile, and swallowed by a family. In this case, maybe I would live to sixty. Still, that is longer than I imagine living a human life.

I would like to be a shelter-providing tree; a low hanging willow that could save people from ice winds. It is the type of tree I needed to survive the street. I think of the pines that protected me when I see a tent in an underpass.

I do not pretend to know how the unsheltered community operates here, but I do see the violence City causes. I talk to a friend who was at the eviction in Lamport Stadium, they tell me of the police parade, the fence that trapped people in, and how they stopped the water from going in. People call this an eviction;

I think it should be called eradication.

In Hometown, the unhoused congregate in Memorial Park due to its position across from a harm reduction non-profit. Here, the tents are like community. The trees watch me hand out homemade meals and art supplies to familiar faces. Maple watches as the first establishment was erected in tent City. Poplar watches as tents expand to every free space in the park.

In Hometown there is the echo. An echo of what is happening in big City – it just takes a few moments to arrive. So, Aspen watches the police tear down tents, time after time. No news outlets report on this, not right away – I only hear from Instagram stories. The trees see the resistance; the Community is built again and again. Residents live to resist, after all, it is safer than the shelter. Although I was never a resident here, I feel a sort of proud reclamation. With weather reaching forty degrees celsius, these trees provide life-saving shade. I receive a text, "they hired a security team," and now I see news coverage. A month after Lamport Stadium it happens in Hometown, only people don't care as much. A news article reports a quote that the new enforcement is in the park for sixteen hours a day – the same ones hired to exterminate the same people from the bus terminal. I watch videos as they stomp down the houses. I feel guilty for recognizing faces and being too far away to do anything.

If I was a tree, I would have watched them put up the wire fence. Just like the bus terminal. Where do people go if they keep kicking them out of public spaces? Surely, they will go somewhere else, and it's a cycle you see – new security, new fence, new resistance. I let tears run down my bark. I think of the half-dead pine, my lungs become bleeding branches.

This is all to say,
I would want to be a tree
that could protect people from wind or heat.

This is also to say,
that the Cities would most certainly cut me down
or fence me away.

What I want you to take away is
people living outside deserve to take up

space.

Meteor Fragmenting

Lindsay Mayhew

Home is a scrapbook of juxtaposition,
a kaleidoscope of memories & becomings
all fragmented,
colourful,
jagged.

I am privileged to be
loved.
I extend my arms to those who raised me &
thank my childhood:
running through creeks,
clean air to breathe,
& birds chirping.
in some ways,
a paradise forged
for me.

if place is part of my identity,
I am painted in the murals on Elgin Street.
I am sidewalk chalked outside SilverCity.
I am calcified on the shoreline of Ramsay.
I am wafting in the scent of brewed coffee in the Lively Tim
Hortons.
Home
is where every person that grew me
exists.
how could I not love
every inch of it?

but Home is also
Sudbury potholes & long Northern winters.
Sudbury running out of things to do on the weekend.
Sudbury searching for arts community & failing to find it.
I find

Home and city have this messy
disordered relationship.
static,
industrial,
buildings crumbling.
"Dear City Council
Give Us Washrooms Please!
Wash Rooms Are a Human Right"

spray painted & censored on Cedar's legal graffiti wall.

I can't help but think about this dis
jointed existence.
we coexist with so many
that experience Home
unsheltered,
punctured by surveillance & invisibility.
tent cities make us uncomfortable,
but we are comfortable turning blind eyes to poverty,
injustice,
death.
Home is tangled in
Sudbury   funding cuts & community losses.
Sudbury   hospital's racialized violence.
Sudbury   trafficking & settler ignorance.
the older I get

I see how ugly community can be.
just small scale examples of institutional problems.
I would call it broken, but
cities built on stolen land have only
ever been
taught
how to take.

remember
this city's scraps are not our future.

Home
made me a person &
poet
so I know we have imagination.
Liberation hums in the spaces of its absence,
winking in and out of existence
everyday
community investment.

what I love is not a building,
a smokestack,
a street name,
a highway,
but this land
& these people are worth
watering.

when I drive down old highway 17
at just the right time
the big nickel reflects golden light & beams
like the sun
& I realize
even this city,
in all its harvested metals,
burns
for revolution.

The Dimensions of Bodies Kept Afloat

Jesse June-Jack

I: The Length Measured To Love

Hoover Dam is 1244 ft long. From the ridges
of its concrete skin to its midpoint in blooming blue sea,
there is an alleyway made of flora. It cracks open

subtle, like ripples when raindrops crash
headfirst into a pond. Water reclaims
itself at center points. You ask where our
midpoint rests, and I point to the zenith
of your cheek, that mahogany brown
dimple heating carrot top red from smiling
so hard. I find myself tearing up. You think our midpoint
rests at the intersection

on Sheppard and Midland. Equidistant to
our houses is a whirlpool
brewed from intersectional bus rides, park
dalliances mid-summer, streams of purple lilacs
coating jacket pockets as summer sun oozes
honey down our skin,

sanguine gods languishing in a tidal wave. In the midway
point of Hoover Dam rests a canoe buoying at 622 ft.
I follow its lead, letting my ribcage
expand into a raft to house you, a crashing wave.

Your smiles strike against bones and cartilage,
wooden boundaries meant to demarcate hope
from despair.

And yet, there you lay
in the midpoint between heaven and earth,
floating alongside me.

But I cannot follow.
My body remains untethered, scattered,
driftwood languishing in ripples
cut by years of self-loathing. Even the sea
is kind to the sailors begging to sink,
pieces of self dispersed,
some forever lost.

The remnants
of your smile crack my breastplate apart, letting
deep blue seep in, terraforming what was once a heart
into an ocean.

II: The Depth Measured To Believe

You can submerge a body of water into a personal memory.
It takes a space in your liver,
squelching against heartbeat pink,
the linings of your body.

Walls soak up cabin pressure, turquoise blue
salting down chiseled stone to perforation,
drowning
is
another
form
of
prayer.

absolution to a holiness that takes every last breath.

Every partition in the photo album hides a sea. Swallowed
in sepia, twirling around the corners, the water drips
into the Styrofoam cup birthday dinners, the half-raised
toasts to good fortune, the late-night wine purchases
to settle midday apprehension. You can drink so much
and never fully drown until you see yourself. The water
in front of the Hoover Dam is 350ft deep
and yet it pales like pail in a thunderstorm

compared to the rage swirling in your lungs.

    Calm child of blue, do you see yourself in the torn puddle,
    amongst the many raindrops, returning body to form?
    Are your memories fledglings, little crest waves
    coasting schools of fishes and flaccid seaweed,
    etchings of details long forgotten, like your uncle's
    grass-churning laugh mid soccer-game appraisal, or
    the way your thumb rubs against the inner glint
    of silver rings, polishing what has never been allowed

to sully itself in the dirt? Calm child of blue,
    are you afraid of yourself when you dream?
    The sea will nest your head against its chest
    and dream softly alongside you,
        as a mother would alongside her newborn.

It knows that drowning can be a prayer and a prison.
You are owed the space to breathe,
for your faith to fill your lungs
without being submerged in longing.

    The sea, that sempiternal nurturing blue,
    will hold you afloat when your body can't
    because even when you find yourself lost,
    memories become answered prayers too.

III: The Height Measured To Live

HOOVER DAM IS 726 FT HIGH. YOUR CAPACITY TO LOVE IS MUCH HIGHER. THE SEA STRETCHES ITS ARMS OUT TO YOU. THERE IS LOVE TO BE SHARED IN ALL THE OCEANS. LOVE AS MUCH AS YOU NEED. LET YOURSELF BE LOVED. THERE IS NO DIVIDING LINE HERE. EVERY END IS A NEW BEGINNING. THE SEA STRETCHES ITS ARMS OUT TO YOU.

W E L C O M E   H O M E

Home

Brennan Gregoire

A cicada's song marked a late August heatwave that hinted September was just around the corner. Some things never change. The sun beat its violence against my shoulders while I watched Junction lap over itself between the foliage of the creek. It didn't quite look the same in the fall; or the winter or spring. It had a peace to it, now. A peace, I'd be waiting another year to see.

Sun rays traced through the power lines, and I was lost in that late summer haze until a blaring slurry truck's horn spiked up, followed by a shout,

"Learn to drive, dumbfuck!"

I smiled a little, hopped off the culvert, and grabbed my bike. I had to get a move on, anyways.

This part of Sudbury wasn't home anymore, but it still felt like it. Afterall, it held most of my firsts; home, school, and friends. All that stuff you think back on when nothing else seems to matter as much. Lately, my mind had been lingering around those cracked asphalt tennis courts, rusty old fences, overgrown laneways, and days spent building dirt jumps behind the school. Even though most of those aren't there anymore, if you look in the right places, you can still make out what's left.

I turned off onto the old railbed where the tracks no longer existed. Just the old railway ties and black-orange slag that was scattered like relics of something that once was. That no longer is. Yet, those sparse rocks mixed with the lush green of the leaves let me know I was home. I hopped off my bike, slid off my backpack, and pulled out a beer. Not like I could bike on the slag and there wasn't much better a place to drink than here. Plus, I'd bet the other guys had already started, and I didn't want to be the only one to roll up sober.

The trail narrowed and the trees grew sparse where the encroaching suburbs pushed further in each year. I came up to a small hill with a stair set that seemed monstrous as a kid. Not so much now, though. At the top was the way to go, at the bottom was my childhood home. I leaned my bike against the railing at the bottom, sat on the step, and opened another drink in the heat of the summer sun and dust clouds from ATVs.

The house looked different. The pines I'd watch from the kitchen table with my sister, while we made faces at each other behind cereal boxes, were cut down. The spreading vines that climbed the brick, now, retreated someplace else. And our little crab apple tree we planted one year was nowhere to be found. Yet, the old baseball field down the street looked the same. I'd take the little victories, I guess.

Could've been the drinks, but staring at the new and the old I couldn't help but relate. There was a part of me that was still in this place but a part that wasn't. While I felt like that kid playing at the bottom of the street, he felt further away each time I came back. The streets became the scenery and the home became a house. The mid-twenties are a strange time. It's like you're waiting to be finished with them but they aren't quite done with you yet. So, I'd keep up the balancing act of the in between while I figured it out, I guess.

A lot of memories came back, sitting there. Mostly good, some bad. Maybe it was the time, the news talking about all those graves found of Indigenous kids. It had me thinking of my Grandfather and what he would've thought.

It was Christmas, sometime. My sister and I tore open our presents like all kids do. There was one that wasn't wrapped, though. My sister pulled off a sheet that was on top of it and underneath was a rabbit. She shrieked, enthused. I wasn't sure what to think of it at first, then came a knock. My Grandfather, with his usual envelope of left-over change, and a bag of KitKats to boot, came in. Everyone chatted away, but I sat in front of the cage and pet the little guy.

"Brennan, do you know what that is," he asked.

"It's a rabbit, like *Thumper*," I said.

"No, it's a wâpos," he said.

"Wabush?" I asked.

"Wah-puss," he enunciated.

I knew about as much as any four-year-old knew about his family. Except Moose Factory was fun to say. My grandfather never talked about it much and I never saw it – *maybe one day, probably not.* The most I heard about the place was from my Mother. She said my Grandmother came over from England after the war and took one look at the place before giving him an ultimatum. Either they left or she was going back home.

A family walked by and shot me, and my beer can, a dirty look. They must've been new around here. I tossed the empty in my pack, grabbed the bike, and headed out. The guys would be wondering where I was by this point.

I turned off the highway and onto some trails near a gravel pit. Night was calling. The sun slumped along the horizon, casting hues of orange and pink across the sky while a chorus of spring peepers came to life in the cool air. I always found myself choosing these sounds over car engines when I could.

I hit the laneway and followed the street to Dan's. Up the driveway, the smell of fire and some chatter filled the air as I watched shadows dance behind the fence. I swung open the gate and joined the party.

"Hey, what's up, dude," Dan said, standing by the fire.

"Eh you cunt," came from Ethan.

"Sup, guys?" I asked.

"Holy fuck," Dan started, "You biked out here?"

"Yeah, man. You know I love a good bike ride," I replied.

"I do enough exercise at work, you know," David added another, "I don't need to be doing anymore when I'm off. How's it going, anyways, you greasy Mexican?"

I set my bike along the fence while the guys chatted away – mostly nonsense with some nostalgia.

We chatted over a few drinks and caught up the way friends do when they're older. It wasn't elementary-school anymore, or high-school for that matter. We didn't get to see each other everyday like we used to - or when we all worked together at the gas station down the street.

Our conversations mixed bits of present and past – always a strong note on the past. Conversations with friends you've known forever never focus on the future; only what used to be.

I didn't see them enough to mind.

"Aren't you heading to Europe soon, Jamie?" Dan asked.

"Yeah," he replied, "going back to see the family."

"I gotta get out there, one day," Dan added, "Canada is good and all, but I'd like to see home."

"You were born here, though," I added.

"Yeah, but it ain't the same," Dan answered, "there's a difference in being where you are and where you're from. And I'd like to see where my grandparents were from."

It'd been fifteen years since my grandfather passed away. I remembered it like it was last week. I was twelve, it was the seventh grade. He was in a senior's home after it was decided he couldn't live on his own anymore. No more change or KitKats. He didn't like it too much; who would? My Mother and Aunts visited that place like clockwork, and I was told he had a real habit of making it a hard job for them. One day after school, and I was the only one home, he called the house.

"Hey big guy," he asked – I was a chubby kid, "is your mom home?"

"No, she's at work, still, I think," I replied, "she should be home soon, though."

"Well, how was your da-,"

"Huh," I answered, paying more attention to the video game I was playing.

"How was your day?" he asked.

"It was okay," I said, "I'm in the middle of something, grandpa. Sorry, I gotta go."

"Okay, love you," I heard as I hung up the phone.

A few days later, after he passed, I cried in my room for not saying I loved him back.

Back outside, after a few drinks too many, I sat on the steps of the deck, puffing on a burnt cigarette filter, and listened to my friends yammer on while they battled with the whiskey.

"Have you seen the bullshit they're saying now?" Dan started, addressing anyone who'd listen.

The summer night, brisk, beautiful, cold.

"Please, baby," his fiancé started, "no politics on the deck."

"Babe, babe, listen," he mumbled.

"Another cigarette would be great," I mumbled, ready for the night's hot take.

"Guys, they're tryna' fuck us again. Like it's our fault that a bunch of kids were found in those graves. How much of it is even true? Like, what do you expect, an apology? I didn't do nothing!"

"Dude, can you just shut the fuck up," I said.

"You're not even that native, Brennan," someone said.

"Alexis," Ethan called, "Dan won't stop."

Alexis grabbed Dan's arm and led him down to the fire.

I had a slight shiver from the cold.

"Alright, that's enough," she said.

"Like I killed those kids, they want to make it seem like it's all our fault for everything," he added, being dragged away by his fiancé.

The party quickly staled on my palate like the thick taste of tobacco. I finished off my drink and said my goodbyes.

"Alright, man," David said, "You sure you wanna bike home?"

"Yeah, man. I don't get to bike at night, much, these days. Work and all, you know," I shrugged.

"Crazy fucker," he added, "still down for Gonga's in the morning?"

"Of course, dude," I added.

"See yah' later," Ethan said, sticking his fist out to me, "cunt," then pulled it back from a fist bump I knew I wasn't getting anyways. I smiled.

The road wasn't so bad at night, not as many people. I watched the familiar houses stare back at me like they did when I was growing up. The cool air mixed with the late summer's dew was a reminder that I wouldn't be doing this again till next year, maybe. When I got to that old culvert by Junction, I tossed down my bike and sat for a little; the words from my friend still buzzed around my mind while I listened to the water.

I wondered what my grandfather would have thought of home when he was here. Would he still see it the same way or was it someplace different now? How much in a life can come and go without any proof that you were there? My mom told me the last words he said to her, though.

"I'm going home."

On nights like this, the wind in the grass, the moon through the trees, the water's whisper, it felt as close as I'd get for now.

Rabbits Chasing Tail

Connor Lafortune

I tell partner that polyamory is sacred; tell them I use that word with my grandfather's tongue. I tell them that sacredness is beauty in bone bearing brilliance. I want to tell my ancestors that my sex is sacred too. Tell my family that my love is shards of glass pressing into skin. Tell my hands not to avoid theirs in public.

bleed, I tell you, bleed.

settler colonial Love is repetition
"I love you"
"I love you"
"I love you"

having to be said every time I see relative

hang up phone

pretend to say it back

it has never been about choice

love has always been hard
rocks tumbling from the mountain
out of my mouth

I spit pebbles on the floor
and hope one of them spells *something*

where to find love in a crumbling cavity?

so I build home instead
prop up the walls with stone and cement
plant seeds in the garden and watch them grow

did you know
blueberry bushes grow bigger
after wildfire

did you know
willow trees keep the metals in their roots
to remove them from the earth

did you know
sword ferns soak up formaldehyde
to purify the air

I thought maybe I too
could grow something out of the dark
could build something out of
t re m bl i ng
foundations

carve furniture from marble
lay bricks of shattered stone
leave room between the c racks
for something else to prosper

sew fences from wire
only to give tomato
something to grow onto

I am beginning to see that home
is something to hold onto
something that holds onto you

I am learning
to let others plant their seeds
to grow along their fences
to let them carve the walls

my friends have started to say
'I love you'
when they leave

I hope someday I can tell them
love has never meant as much to me
as home

I hope someday I can tell them
that they have etched their name in foundation
that they are part of home

I hope someday I can tell everyone
so much more
about my home

I have come into myself this week. Decided that nimazhiwe does not only mean to have sex but to take up space in community. I sometimes forget that vulgarity is seen negatively in Western light. *Poonjegay* means to dip meat in grease; means to relay the body from one wet extremity to the other; to bask in the brash and blatant. Young nishnaabs say *poonj* to mean sex and sacred. To reclaim the place of a fearless ferocious fuck. To unpack boundaries of private property proclamations.

I do not hoard love
I harvest it in baskets
keep them open on my shelf
spread fields of it in my yard

on days I do not see myself as a love poet

I

re tie the knots
re tie the knots
re tie the knots

until I am macrame
tightrope walker
kinky boy scout

tell myself I am made of maple forest

until I see
that all of my love-me-nots
have seeded to sapling

to cut into lodge
to make into womb
to hold all of my healing

I am   breathe of first air
I am   light over hidden eyelids
I am   otter
                        reaching out

I tell partner
that we only let family
    and lovers
    and own hands
braid our hair

that kind of closeness can only be forged
                                                            through blood
                                                            and bond
                                                            and memory

I want them to be daffodils petals
embedded in my scalp
seedlings of dense trees
planted in my root
                systems

I tell partner we are poly like rabbits chasing tails

like untamed,   unnamed,   undomesticated love

we are sacred like savages spurning shame

The Dragon

Ra'anaa Yaminah Ekundayo

I inhale
lungs full
of breathless embers
as ominous clouds warn
and my heavy heart wanes

chest tight
fists clenched
freedom in my eyes

sleepless nights
seek rejuvenating days
body cool to the touch
but heat on my lips

their wise lies
and tumultuous truths
age and fade

our wildest dreams
take shape

deceitful porcelain walls
shatter and break
as I breathe fire
their kingdom set ablaze

burn out their deception
as I speak
a crackle and spark
igniting my rage

engulfed in flames
blinded by smoke
their eyes water
delicate ivory tears

no longer battered
captured or shackled
I am the dragon freed
by words set aflame

Firestorm

Michelle Delorme

The summer that I am afraid of fire, clouds swell into a smoke-tinged anvil
Bloodred sun screaming through the haze of charred particles
Drought as tinder, wildfire mast year ignites and erupts
Climate Change Pyrocumulonimbus
Carbon dioxide-a ugmented firestorm
Inferno licking up black spruce,
Tamarack, and Jack pine
Spikes of worry
Plumes of smoke
Forest
Funeral
Pyres
Blaze
Scorch
Incinerate

Across the blackened landscape, green seedlings poke through dust and ash; a young forest reawakened.

In The Aftermath of Apocalypse

Connor Lafortune and Lindsay Mayhew

The world's pseudonym is Devouring
We live in the underbelly, crowded
It ingested all it could stomach, releasing
only
what we demand

We are liver
demanding nothing
but change

What is a good life without
capital?
What is currency without
paper or plastic?

We take
take
take
the shape of snakes
embedded in the earth's skin

We used to measure wealth
by what we could give:
Our time
knowledge
skills
Now
we give nothing but a hand
shaking over contract
hoping His nails can screw them over
this time

What
is a nation
without

its genocide?

What
is genocide
if not
a nation
calling it
co existence?

What is history
if not
repeating?
repeating?
repeating?

A citizen is like its nation
Idolized, Independent, Individual,
complicit
Settler is the right word
for something seemingly passive
but to settle
is a choice to be empty, endlessly
Devouring & devoured
to forever feast on the famished

I was born in an exemplary country
Yes
Canada is the prime example
of how to get away with murder
to be murdered again
and never get away

I was born in a country exempt from accountability
Yes
Canada is a prime number counting itself over and over
again
forgetting First is a People they lose count of

What is land if not future
empire

What is future if not empire
being burnt down

I am flesh on fire
sinew sewn to oil sands
veins bleeding into wells
waiting for bones to implode

fracked into fragments

What is history
if not
if not
if not
Possibility
never lacks
imagination simply fails

What am I if not mouth
screaming between swallows?
What are we if not dovetailing New
World with each breath?

What are you if not pigeon
following the flock?

What if we escape this barren soil
and pierce acidic cloud cover
marking the sky with distrails
rendering
the horizon with evidence of our living
breaking barriers of blaze and smoke to breathe

again

The world's pseudonym is Devastate
We live in the aftermath of apocalypse
waiting for ruins to flourish
petals of revelations
knowing it will all collapse

Acknowledgments

We would first like to extend our deep appreciation to each of our contributors. You are the heart of this creation. Your art and your stories are valuable, powerful, and will continue to inspire. Thank you for sharing a piece of yourselves with us and our readers.

To our friend and talented cover artist, Grant Neegan (@featurelessdesigns). Your creativity is boundless and we are honoured to have your work incorporated in the collection. We are forever grateful and in awe of your incredible artistry.

This collection would not be possible without Heather Campbell and Latitude 46 Publishing. To Heather, who was there at the birth of *A Thousand Tiny Awakenings,* and filled our spirits with encouragement, advice, and above all else, believed in us and our vision.

Dear young writers, continue to awaken the world around you.

A Thousand Tiny Awakenings was inspired by poets, theorists, and artists alike. Elizabeth Grosz, Billy-Ray Belcourt, and many others, thank you for your revolutionary contributions to the world.

To our dear readers, thank you. Change starts with you.

Author Bios

Waed Hasan is a Palestinian refugee and PhD candidate at the University of Guelph. Hasan is an emerging scholar in Palestinian Studies and Critical Refugee Studies. Her research focuses on the establishment of Refugee Poetics as an inclusive decolonial genre to broaden the scope of literary reading and understanding of refugee experiences. Hasan has over eight years of experience in various academic positions including teaching assistant and learning specialist. Her creative work can be found in several journals and publications.

Chimdi Kingsley-Emereuwa (Soulful Echo) is an artist and has been writing for the past 3 years. Chimdi performs poems to convey emotions that are penned down. With an undying passion for art, Chimdi hopes to tell real stories that view humanity as a unified identity, and every stride to be a better artist brings forth Chimdi's undying passion for art, love for humanity, and the ability to be the change.

Nicole Robitaille is a Ghanaian-Canadian writer living in North Bay, Ontario. She has honours BA degrees in English and Psychology from Nipissing University, and has been published in Room Magazine, The Brooklyn Review, and Antilang.

Ra'anaa Yaminah Ekundayo is an emerging multimedia visual activist scholar whose practice extends between Tiohtià:ke (Montreal, QC) and N'Swakamok (Sudbury, ON). Their work explores the intersection of art and activism, particularly contemplating the entanglement of Black identity, community, and futurity. Co-founder and Chair of Black Lives Matter Sudbury, Ra'anaa strives for an active decolonization of every facet of their life, supporting calls to defund the police, abolish the prison industrial complex, and for liberation in our lifetime. They have taken on many leadership roles, as an artist, activist, and academic, creating space for people of colour and continually promoting anti-racist practices and social justice. Ra'anaa is impassioned by community-engaged art and the notion that art should be inherently accessible. A Black queer cultural curator, Ra'anaa's work embodies Black joy and love, focusing on Black identity, and community care, infused with elements of Afrofuturism.

A recent graduate of the University of Maine with her Master's in English, **Sydney Read** currently lives in Bangor, Maine, with her partner Chris and their cat and dog. She loves reading and writing poems that foreground reciprocity between reader and world, and cause her to orient herself toward that connection. Her successfully defended thesis, titled, "Reciproesis: On Making-with the More-than-human," is a critical exploration of what it means to consciously orient oneself toward the natural world through the writing and reading of poetry. When she's not writing, you can find her reading, playing video games, or looking hopefully up at the sky.

Kay Kassirer (they/them) is a spoken word poet whose autobiographical poetry focuses on gender & sexuality, grief, disability, and sex work. Kay has toured internationally performing at venues like Buddies in Bad Times Theatre, Busboys and Poets, and the Bowery Poetry Club. They have competed at over a dozen national and international poetry slam festivals earning their place on several competitive final stages. Kay curated and edited 'A Whore's Manifesto: An Anthology of Writing and Artwork by Sex Workers' published by Thornapple Press. Their work has been featured in numerous places, including Button Poetry, Write About Now, and Arc Poetry Magazine.

Carson Bohdi (any pronouns) is an Author, Poet, Content Creator, and awkward duck from Toronto, Canada. They are most well known for the video series, "Recovering Alcoholic Reacts" on Youtube. Their first poetry collection, REQUIEM, was self-published in 2022 and highlights their journey with addiction and gender identity. They continue to reside in Toronto with their rubber ducks.

Lisa Shen is a writer and spoken word artist, and the 2023-2025 Youth Poet Laureate of the City of Mississauga. She placed second at the 2023 Canadian Individual Poetry Slam. Her work has appeared on *CBC Radio, TEDx,* and *Rattle.* Her debut chapbook *A Story Ending in Redwoods* is forthcoming with Anstruther Press.

Tyler Hein is a Finnish-Canadian writer from Sudbury, Ontario who now resides in Vancouver. He holds an MFA in creative writing from the University of British Columbia. His work has been published across the world, most recently in *This Magazine, Freefall,* and *Outcrop Poetry*. More of his work can be found at tylerhein.ca.

Michelle Delorme, an environmental scientist from Sault Ste. Marie, Ontario, explores themes of grief, ecology, and climate change in her poetry. Inspired by the landscapes of Lake Superior, her work intertwines personal reflections with ecological knowledge, inviting readers to contemplate our connection to the Earth and the importance of environmental justice.

Blaine Thornton is a non-binary community-based writer and installation artist from Sudbury, Ontario. Their book, *Here's To Letting Go*, was awarded the 2023 OCAD U Medal for Creative Writing. They work in community arts and are interested in how writing can be used as a tool for self-healing and creating vibrant artistic spaces for people to experiment in.

Jesse June-Jack is a 22-year-old Afro-Canadian written and spoken word poet based in Toronto, Canada. He has performed with organizations such as Unity Charity, Word Is Bond, RISE, Poetry Saved Our Lives, etc. He has also been published in Block Party Magazine, BAM Youth Slam, the Toronto Young Voices Magazine, and an animated television project called DREAMS IN VANTABLACK, which can be found on YouTube/ CBC Gem.

Brennan Gregoire (he/him) is an avid reader and writer from Sudbury Ontario. Spending most of his time around the woods and outskirts, he brings the world he sees to life through writing. This is his second publication, his first being with Sulphur Literary Journal.

About the Editors

Connor Lafortune is from Dokis First Nation on Robinson Huron Treaty territory of 1850 in Northeastern Ontario. He works primarily in Life Promotion, harm-reduction, mental health, and Indigenous education. He completed his Bachelor's Degree at Nipissing University with a Double Honors Major in Indigenous Studies and Gender Equality and Social Justice. He is currently in the Masters in Indigenous Relations at Laurentian University. Connor is Anishinaabek, Queer, and Francophone; he uses his understanding of the world to shape his creations as a writer, spoken word poet, and musician. Connor often combines the written word with traditional Indigenous beadwork and sewing to recreate the stories of colonization, showcase resilience, and imagine a new future. He recently released a single in collaboration with Juno Award winner G.R. Gritt titled "Qui crie au loup ? ft. Connor Lafortune." Above all else, Connor is an activist, a shkaabewis *(helper)*, and a compassionate human being.

Lindsay Mayhew (she/her) is a spoken word artist and writer from Sudbury, Ontario. She recently graduated with a Master's in English Literature from the University of Guelph. Lindsay is the multi-year champion of Wordstock Sudbury's poetry slam and has featured in events across Ontario, including JAYU Canada, Hamilton's 10th Fashion Week, and Nuit Blanche. She represented Canada in the 2024 Womxn of the World poetry slam. Lindsay's written work is featured in the *Literary Review of Canada*, *Moria*, and *Sulphur*. Her spoken word and written work combines art, emotion, and theory to voice mental health advocacy, healing, and feminist futures.